Informing the legislative debate since 1914 _____

U.S.-Mexico Economic Relations:
Trends, Issues, and Implications

M. Angeles Villarreal
Specialist in International Trade and Finance

July 1, 2014

Congressional Research Service

7-5700

www.crs.gov

RL32934

Summary

During the remainder of the 113th Congress, policymakers will likely maintain an interest in Mexico on issues related to cross-border trade, Mexico's participation in the Trans-Pacific Partnership (TPP) agreement negotiations, energy sector and other reforms in Mexico, economic conditions in Mexico, migration, and border issues. Congress may take a more active interest in the opening of Mexico's energy sector to foreign and private investment for the first time in 76 years. President Peña Nieto began his presidency with an ambitious reform agenda. In December 2013, he signed into law a constitutional amendment that will allow oil companies to gain access to untapped oil reserves in Mexico, which are estimated to be as high as 113 billion barrels. The Mexican Congress must approve secondary legislation to implement the historic reforms. Most industry experts agree that Mexico's state-owned oil monopoly, *Petróleos Mexicanos* (Pemex) lacks the financial and technical resources to operate its existing fields efficiently or to expand into new fields.

The bilateral economic and trade relationship with Mexico is of interest to U.S. policymakers because of Mexico's proximity to the United States, the high level of bilateral trade, and the strong cultural and economic ties that connect the two countries. Also, it is of national interest for the United States to have a prosperous and democratic Mexico as a neighboring country. Mexico is the United States' third-largest trading partner, while the United States is, by far, Mexico's largest trading partner. Mexico ranks third as a source of U.S. imports, after China and Canada, and second, after Canada, as an export market for U.S. goods and services. The United States is the largest source of foreign direct investment (FDI) in Mexico.

The United States and Mexico have strong economic ties through the North American Free Trade Agreement (NAFTA), which has been in effect since 1994. Prior to NAFTA, Mexico had followed a strong protectionist policy for decades until it began to unilaterally liberalize its trade regime in the late 1980s. Not all trade-related job gains and losses since NAFTA can be entirely attributed to the agreement because of the numerous factors that affect trade, such as Mexico's trade liberalization efforts, economic conditions, and currency fluctuations. NAFTA may have accelerated the ongoing trade and investment trends that were already taking place at the time. Most studies show that the net economic effects of NAFTA on both countries have been small but positive, though there have been adjustment costs to some sectors within both countries.

In June 2012, President Barack Obama announced that the nine countries involved in the TPP negotiations had extended an invitation to Mexico and Canada to join negotiations for the proposed multilateral free trade agreement. The proposed TPP would likely enhance the economic links Mexico already has with the United States and Canada under NAFTA. This could include further reduction of barriers to trade and the negotiation of key issues in areas such as agriculture, intellectual property rights protection, government procurement, regulatory cohesion, and others.

The United States, Mexico, and Canada have made efforts since 2005 to increase cooperation on economic and security issues through various endeavors, most notably by participating in the North American Leaders Summits. The most recent Summit was hosted by President Enrique Peña Nieto in Mexico on February 19, 2014. The three leaders discussed issues on the economic well-being, safety, and security of North America and issued a joint statement renewing their commitment to regulatory cooperation in key areas or interest.

Contents

Figures

Tables

Appendixes

Contacts

Introduction

The bilateral economic relationship with Mexico is of key interest to the United States because of Mexico's proximity, the high volume of trade with Mexico, and the strong cultural and economic ties between the two countries. The United States and Mexico share many common interests related to trade, investment, and regulatory cooperation. The two countries share a 2,000 mile border and have extensive interconnections through the Gulf of Mexico. There are also links through migration, tourism, environmental issues, health concerns, and family and cultural relationships.

The remainder of the 113th Congress will likely maintain an active interest in Mexico on issues related to Mexico's economic reform measures, especially in the energy sector; cross-border trade between the two countries; Mexico's participation in the Trans-Pacific Partnership (TPP) agreement negotiations; migration; and other border issues. Congress may continue to take an interest in the economic policies of Mexico's President, Enrique Peña Nieto. Since entering into office on December 1, 2012, Peña Nieto has advocated numerous economic and political reforms that include, among other measures, opening up the energy sector to private investment, countering monopolistic practices, passing fiscal reform, making farmers more productive, and increasing infrastructure investment.[1] Peña Nieto also endorses an active international trade policy aimed at increasing Mexico's trade with Asia, South America, and other markets. His government is taking an active role in the negotiations for a TPP.[2]

This report provides an overview of U.S.-Mexico economic relations, trade trends, the Mexican economy, NAFTA, and trade issues between the United States and Mexico. It will be updated as events warrant.

U.S.-Mexico Economic Relations

Mexico is one of the United States' key trading partners, ranking second among U.S. export markets and third in total U.S. trade (imports plus exports). Under the North American Free Trade Agreement (NAFTA), the United States and Mexico have developed significant economic ties. Trade between the two countries more than tripled since the agreement was implemented in 1994. Through NAFTA, the United States, Mexico, and Canada form one of the world's largest free trade areas, with about one-third of the world's total gross domestic product (GDP). Mexico has the second-largest economy in Latin America after Brazil. It has a population of 116 million people, making it the most populous Spanish-speaking country in the world and the third-most populous country in the Western Hemisphere (after the United States and Brazil).

Mexico's gross domestic product (GDP) was an estimated $1.3 trillion in 2013, slightly less than 8% of U.S. GDP of $16.8 trillion. Per capita income in Mexico is significantly lower than in the

---

[1] For more information, see CRS Report R42917, *Mexico: Background and U.S. Relations*, by Clare Ribando Seelke, and CRS Report R43313, *Mexico's Oil and Gas Sector: Background, Reform Efforts, and Implications for the United States*, coordinated by Clare Ribando Seelke.

[2] For more information on the Trans-Pacific Partnership negotiations, see CRS Report R42694, *The Trans-Pacific Partnership (TPP) Negotiations and Issues for Congress*, coordinated by Ian F. Fergusson.

United States. In 2013, Mexico's per capita GDP in purchasing power parity[3] was $17,990, or 66% lower than U.S. per capita GDP of $53,104 (see **Table 1**). Ten years earlier, in 2003, Mexico's per capita GDP in purchasing power parity was $10,887, or 71% lower than the U.S. amount of $39,652. Although there is a notable income disparity with the United States, Mexico's per capita GDP is relatively high by global standards, and falls within the World Bank's upper-middle income category.[4] Mexico's economy relies heavily on the United States as an export market. The value of exports equaled 32% of Mexico's GDP in 2013, as shown in **Table 1**, and approximately 80% of Mexico's exports are headed to the United States.

Table 1. Key Economic Indicators for Mexico and the United States

	Mexico		**United States**	
	2003	**2013**[a]	**2003**	**2013**[a]
Population (millions)	104	116	290	316
Nominal GDP (US$ billions)[b]	713	1,259	11,512	16,800
Nominal GDP, PPP[c] Basis (US$ billions)	1,129	2,091	11,512	16,800
Per Capita GDP (US$)	6,877	10,830	39,653	53,104
Per Capita GDP in $PPPs	10,887	17,990	39,653	53,104
Nominal exports of goods & services (US$ billions)	178	400	1,043	2,260
Exports of goods & services as % of GDP[d]	24%	32%	9%	14%
Nominal imports of goods & services (US$ billions)	188	409	1,544	2,757
Imports of goods & services as % of GDP[d]	26%	33%	13%	16%

Source: Compiled by CRS based on data from Economist Intelligence Unit (EIU) online database.

a. Some figures for 2013 are estimates.

b. Nominal GDP is calculated by EIU based on figures from World Bank and World Development Indicators.

c. PPP refers to purchasing power parity, which reflects the purchasing power of foreign currencies in U.S. dollars.

d. Exports and Imports as % of GDP derived by EIU.

U.S.-Mexico Trade

The United States is, by far, Mexico's leading partner in merchandise trade, while Mexico is the United States' third-largest trade partner after China and Canada. Mexico ranks second among U.S. export markets after Canada, and is the third-leading supplier of U.S. imports. U.S. trade with Mexico increased rapidly since NAFTA entered into force in January 1994. U.S. exports to Mexico increased from $54.8 billion in 1994 to $226.2 billion in 2013, an increase of 313%. Imports from Mexico increased from $51.6 billion in 1994 to $280.5 billion in 2013, an increase

---

[3] Purchasing power parity (PPP) reflects the purchasing power of foreign currencies in their own markets in U.S. dollars.

[4] The World Bank utilizes a method for classifying world economies based on gross national product (GNP). Mexico is one of 48 economies classified as upper-middle-income, or countries which have a per capita GNP of $3,946 to $12,195 per year. The United States is one of 69 economies classified as a high-income, or countries which have a per capita GNP of more than $12,195 per year.

of 444% (see **Figure 1**). In services, the United States had a surplus of $12.2 billion in 2012. U.S. exports in services to Mexico totaled $27.4 billion in 2012, while U.S. imports totaled $15.1 billion.[5]

The merchandise trade balance with Mexico went from a surplus of $3.1 billion in 1994 to a widening deficit that reached a peak of $74.3 billion in 2007. In 2013, the merchandise trade deficit with Mexico was $54.3 billion. In 2013, 14% of total U.S. merchandise exports were destined for Mexico, and 12% of U.S. merchandise imports came from Mexico.

As stated previously, Mexico relies heavily on the United States as an export market; this reliance has diminished very slightly over the years. The percentage of Mexico's total exports going to the United States decreased from 83% in 1996 to 79% in 2013. Mexico's share of the U.S. market has lost ground since 2003 when China surpassed Mexico as the second-leading supplier of U.S. imports. The U.S. share of Mexico's import market has also decreased. Between 1996 and 2013, the U.S. share of Mexico's total imports decreased from 75% to 49%. China is Mexico's second-leading supplier of imports, accounting for 16% of Mexico's total imports in 2013.[6]

Not all of the increase in U.S.-Mexico trade since the 1990s can be attributable to NAFTA. Other variables, such as exchange rates and economic conditions, also affect trade. For example, Mexico's currency crisis of 1995 limited the purchasing power of the Mexican people in the years that followed and also made products from Mexico less expensive for the U.S. market. Several studies between 2003 and 2004 on the effects of NAFTA found that U.S. trade deficits with Mexico were largely driven by macroeconomic trends, and, in the case of U.S.-Mexico trade, caused by the respective business cycles in Mexico and the United States.[7]

---

[5] U.S. Bureau of Economic Analysis interactive statistics, available at http://www.bea.gov.

[6] Based on data from *Global Trade Atlas*.

[7] For more information on the effects of NAFTA, see CRS Report R42965, *NAFTA at 20: Overview and Trade Effects*, by M. Angeles Villarreal and Ian F. Fergusson.

Figure 1. U.S. Merchandise Trade with Mexico

(U.S. $ in billions)

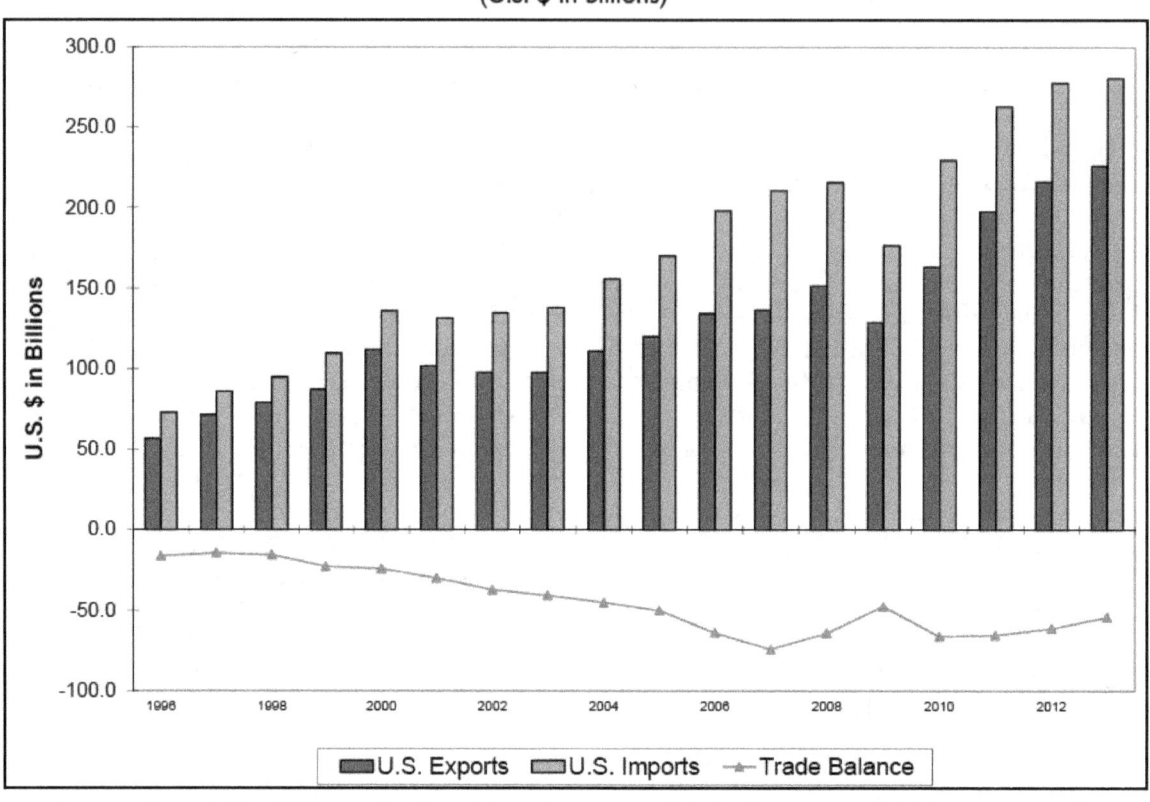

Source: Compiled by CRS using the United States International Trade Commission (USITC) Interactive Tariff and Trade DataWeb at http://dataweb.usitc.gov.

The leading U.S. import item from Mexico in 2013 was motor vehicles ($40.1 billion), followed by motor vehicle parts ($35.2 billion), oil and gas ($32.0 billion), computer equipment ($15.0 billion), and audio and video equipment ($13.8 billion), as shown in **Table 2**. After sharp decreases in 2009 caused by the global economic downturn, U.S. imports from Mexico have increased. Imports increased from $176.5 billion in 2009 to $280.5 billion in 2013.

The leading U.S. export item to Mexico in 2013 was motor vehicle parts ($21.1 billion), followed by petroleum and coal products ($19.3 billion), computer equipment ($14.8 billion), semiconductors and other electronic components ($13.0 billion), and basic chemicals ($10.1 billion), as shown in **Table 3**.

Table 2. U.S. Imports from Mexico: 2009-2013

(U.S. $ in billions)

Items (NAIC 4-digit)	2009	2010	2011	2012	2013	% Total in 2013
Motor vehicles	18.4	27.5	30.5	35.3	40.1	14%
Motor vehicle parts	15.5	23.6	28.5	33.3	36.2	13%
Oil and gas	22.2	29.5	39.8	37.3	32.0	11%
Computer equipment	7.6	13.6	14.5	16.0	14.8	5%
Audio and video equipment	15.7	16.5	14.7	14.2	13.8	5%
Other	97.2	119.0	135.0	141.4	143.5	51%
Total	176.5	229.7	263.1	277.7	280.5	

Source: Compiled by CRS using USITC Interactive Tariff and Trade DataWeb at http://dataweb.usitc.gov: North American Industrial Classification (NAIC) 4-digit level.

Note: Nominal U.S. dollars.

Table 3. U.S. Exports to Mexico: 2009-2013

(U.S. $ in Billions)

Items (NAIC 4-digit)	2009	2010	2011	2012	2013	% Total in 2013
Motor vehicle parts	9.8	14.1	16.9	19.6	21.1	9%
Petroleum and coal products	6.6	11.9	20.1	20.8	19.3	9%
Computer equipment	7.4	9.9	13.4	14.5	14.8	7%
Semiconductors and other electronic components	8.9	11.8	10.8	11.4	13.0	6%
Basic chemicals	6.2	7.1	9.1	10.1	10.1	4%
Other	90.0	108.5	127.3	140.0	147.8	65%
Total	129.0	163.3	197.5	216.3	226.2	

Source: Compiled by CRS using USITC Interactive Tariff and Trade DataWeb at http://dataweb.usitc.gov: NAIC 4-digit level.

Note: Nominal U.S. dollars.

Bilateral Foreign Direct Investment

Foreign direct investment (FDI) has been an integral part of the economic relationship between the United States and Mexico since NAFTA implementation. The United States is the largest source of FDI in Mexico. The stock of U.S. FDI increased from $17.0 billion in 1994 to $101.0 billion in 2012. Mexican FDI in the United States is much lower than U.S. investment in Mexico. In 2012, the stock of Mexican FDI in the United States totaled $14.9 billion (see **Table 4**).

Table 4. U.S.-Mexican Foreign Direct Investment Positions: 1994-2012 Historical Cost Basis

(U.S. $ in millions)

Year	Mexican FDI in the U.S.	U.S. FDI in Mexico
1994	2,069	16,968
1995	1,850	16,873
1996	1,641	19,351
1997	3,100	24,050
1998	2,055	26,657
1999	1,999	37,151
2000	7,462	39,352
2001	6,645	52,544
2002	7,829	56,303
2003	9,022	56,851
2004	7,592	63,384
2005	3,595	73,687
2006	5,310	82,965
2007	8,478	91,046
2008	8,420	87,443
2009	11,111	84,047
2010	10,970	85,751
2011	13,051	90,795
2012	14,883	101,030

Source: U.S. Department of Commerce, Bureau of Economic Analysis.

The sharp rise in U.S. investment in Mexico since NAFTA is also a result of the liberalization of Mexico's restrictions on foreign investment in the late 1980s and the early 1990s. Prior to the mid-1980s, Mexico had a very protective policy that restricted foreign investment and controlled the exchange rate to encourage domestic growth, affecting the entire industrial sector. Mexico's trade liberalization measures and economic reform in the late 1980s represented a sharp shift in policy and helped bring in a steady increase of FDI flows into Mexico. NAFTA provisions on foreign investment helped to lock in the reforms and increase investor confidence. Under NAFTA, Mexico gave U.S. and Canadian investors nondiscriminatory treatment of their investments as well as investor protection. NAFTA may have encouraged U.S. FDI in Mexico by increasing investor confidence, but much of the growth may have occurred anyway because Mexico likely would have continued to liberalize its foreign investment laws with or without the agreement.

Nearly half of total FDI investment in Mexico is in the manufacturing industry, of which the maquiladora industry forms a major part. (See "Mexico's Export-Oriented Assembly Plants" below.) In Mexico, the industry has helped attract investment from countries such as the United States that have a relatively large amount of capital. For the United States, the industry is important because U.S. companies are able to locate their labor-intensive operations in Mexico and lower their labor costs in the overall production process.

The drug violence has taken a toll on investor confidence in Mexico, especially for those who have not done business in the country previously.[8] However, the resilience of the U.S. economy and the expected growth in U.S. GDP in 2014 may have a positive effect on business activity and a slight positive effect on foreign direct investment.[9] In February 2014, Moody's Investors Service upgraded Mexico's government bond ratings. The upgrade may have a positive effect on investor confidence. Moody's investors service stated that the upgrade of Mexico's sovereign rating was driven by the following four factors linked to the reform package: 1) approval of a comprehensive reform agenda, which reflects political will to address long-standing structural issues; 2) improved medium-term economic prospects associated with higher potential growth that is likely to result from the reform package; 3) a strengthened fiscal outlook that incorporates higher government savings and additional buffers; and 4) an overall credit profile similar to that of other equally rated countries.[10]

Mexico's Export-Oriented Assembly Plants

Mexico's export-oriented assembly plants are closely linked to U.S.-Mexico trade in various labor-intensive industries such as auto parts and electronic goods. These plants generate a large amount of trade with the United States, and a majority of the plants have U.S. parent companies. Foreign-owned assembly plants, which originated under Mexico's maquiladora program in the 1960s,[11] account for a substantial share of Mexico's trade with the United States. The border region with the United States has the highest concentration of assembly plants and workers. Prior to NAFTA, a maquiladora was limited to selling up to 50% of the previous year's export production to the domestic market. Most maquiladoras currently export the majority of their production to the U.S. market.

Private industry groups have stated that these operations help U.S. companies remain competitive in the world marketplace by producing goods at competitive prices. In addition, the proximity of Mexico to the United States allows production to have a high degree of U.S. content in the final product, which could help sustain jobs in the United States. Critics of these types of operations argue that they have a negative effect on the economy because they take jobs from the United States and help depress the wages of low-skilled U.S. workers.

---

[8] IHS Global Insight, Mexico Country Outlook: Capital Investment, updated on February 19, 2014.

[9] Ibid.

[10] Moody's Investors Service, "Moody's upgrades Mexico's sovereign rating to A3 from Baa1; Stable Outlook," February 5, 2014.

[11] Mexico's export-oriented industries began with the maquiladora program established in the 1960s by the Mexican government, which allowed foreign-owned businesses to set up assembly plants in Mexico to produce for export. Maquiladoras could import intermediate materials duty-free with the condition that 20% of the final product be exported. The percentage of sales allowed to the domestic market increased over time as Mexico liberalized its trade regime. U.S. tariff treatment of maquiladora imports played a significant role in the industry. Under HTS provisions 9802.00.60 and 9802.00.80, the portion of an imported good that was of U.S. origin entered the United States duty-free. Duties were assessed only on the value added abroad. After NAFTA, North American rules of origin determine duty-free status. Recent changes in Mexican regulations on export-oriented industries merged the maquiladora industry and Mexican domestic assembly-for-export plants into one program called the Maquiladora Manufacturing Industry and Export Services (IMMEX).

Some observers believe that the correlation in maquiladora growth after 1993 is directly due to NAFTA, but in reality it was a combination of factors that contributed to growth. Trade liberalization, wages, and economic conditions, both in the United States and Mexico, all affected the growth of Mexican export-oriented assembly plants. Although some provisions in NAFTA may have encouraged growth in certain sectors, manufacturing activity has been more influenced by the strength of the U.S. economy and relative wages in Mexico.

Regulations for Mexican Manufacturing Plants

Changes in Mexican regulations on export-oriented industries after NAFTA merged the maquiladora industry and Mexican domestic assembly-for-export plants into one program called the Maquiladora Manufacturing Industry and Export Services (IMMEX). In 2001, the North American rules of origin determined the duty-free status for a given import and replaced the previous special tariff provisions that applied only to maquiladora operations. The initial maquiladora program ceased to exist and the same trade rules applied to all assembly operations in Mexico.

NAFTA rules for the maquiladora industry were implemented in two phases, with the first phase covering the period 1994-2000, and the second phase starting in 2001. During the initial phase, NAFTA regulations continued to allow the maquiladora industry to import products duty-free into Mexico, regardless of the country of origin of the products. This phase also allowed maquiladora operations to increase maquiladora sales into the domestic market. Phase II made a significant change to the industry in that the new North American rules of origin determined duty-free status for U.S. and Canadian products exported to Mexico for maquiladoras. The elimination of duty-free imports by maquiladoras from non-NAFTA countries under NAFTA caused some initial uncertainty for the companies with maquiladora operations. Maquiladoras that were importing from third countries, such as Japan or China, would have to pay applicable tariffs on those goods under the new rules.

Mexico had another program for export-oriented assembly plants called the Program for Temporary Imports to Promote Exports (PITEX) that was established in 1990 to allow qualifying domestic producers to compete with maquiladoras. In 2007, a new set of government regulations on export-oriented industries merged the maquiladora industry and PITEX plants into the Maquiladora Manufacturing Industry and Export Services, or IMMEX. Industry data regarding Mexico's export-oriented assembly plants no longer distinguish maquiladora plants from other Mexican manufacturing plants.

Worker Remittances to Mexico

Remittances are one of the three highest sources of foreign currency for Mexico, along with oil and tourism. Most remittances to Mexico come from workers in the United States who send money back to their relatives in Mexico. Mexico receives the largest amount of remittances in Latin America. Remittances are often a stable financial flow for some regions in Mexico as workers in the United States make efforts to send money to family members. Most of the remittances going to Mexico go to southern states in Mexico where poverty levels are high.

Studies indicate that women are the primary recipients of the money, and usually use it for basic needs such as rent, food, medicine, or utilities.[12]

Annual remittances to Mexico decreased from $22.4 billion in 2012 to $21.7 billion in 2013, as shown in **Table 5**.[13] In 2009 remittances experienced a sharp decline of 15.2%, likely due to the global financial crisis. Prior to this, remittances to Mexico had been increasing rapidly. Between 1996 and 2007, remittances increased from $4.2 billion to $25.1 billion, an increase of over 500%. The annual growth rate reached a high of 54.3% in 2003, and then continued at a slower rate until 2008, when the rate of growth declined. The drop in remittances could be related to changes in migration flows as well to increases in the exchange rate between the Mexican peso and the U.S. dollar.[14]

Electronic transfers and money orders are the most popular methods to send money to Mexico. The rapid increase in remittances during the late 1990s through the mid-2000s can be attributed to numerous factors, but it was also largely influenced by considerable reductions in transaction fees charged by banks. In the 1990s, these fees were as high as 8%, and went down as low as 2.5% in 2003.[15] The Inter-American Development Bank reported that the average cost to send $200 was 6.0% in 2010.[16]

Table 5. Percent Changes in Remittances to Mexico

(U.S. $ in billions)

	2002	2003	2004	2005	2006	2007	2008	2009	2010	2011	2012	2013
Amount	9.8	15.1	18.3	21.7	25.6	26.1	25.1	21.3	21.3	22.8	22.4	21.7
% Change	10.2%	54.3%	21.1%	18.3%	17.9%	1.9%	-3.5%	-15.2%	0.0%	7.0%	-1.8%	-3.1%

Source: Compiled by CRS using data from the Inter-American Development Bank, Multilateral Investment Fund; and Mexico's Central Bank.

Worker remittance flows to Mexico have an important impact on the Mexican economy, in some regions more than others. Some studies on remittance flows to Mexico report that in southern Mexican states, remittances mostly or completely cover general consumption and/or housing. A significant portion of the money received by households goes for food, clothing, health care, and other household expenses. Some remittances mat be used for capital invested in microenterprises throughout urban Mexico.[17] The economic impact of remittance flows is concentrated in the poorer states of Mexico.

---

[12] Inter-American Development Bank (IDB), "Mexico and Remittances," March 16, 2010, available at http://www.iadb.org/mif.

[13] See http://www.banxico.org.mx.

[14] IDB, Multilateral Investment Fund, *Remittances to Latin America and the Caribbean in 2012: Differing Behavior Across Subregions,* 2012.

[15] Federal Reserve Bank of Dallas, "Workers' Remittances to Mexico," *El Paso Business Frontier*, 2004.

[16] Inter-American Development Bank, "Mexico and Remittances," 2010.

[17] The Federal Reserve Bank of Dallas report "Workers' Remittances to Mexico" (2004) evaluated the economic impact of worker remittances to Mexico and cites a number of reports by the World Bank and the Mexican government.

Regulatory Cooperation

The United States, Mexico, and Canada have made efforts since 2005 to increase cooperation on security and economic issues through various endeavors, most notably by participating in trilateral summits known as the North American Leaders Summits. The most recent summit took place on February 19, 2014 in Toluca, Mexico, with an agenda focused on immigration, energy, and commerce. Current bilateral efforts pursed by the Obama Administration with Canada and Mexico have built upon the accomplishments of the working groups formed under the former Security and Prosperity Partnership of North America (SPP) established in 2005 under the Bush Administration. Proponents of North American competitiveness and security cooperation view the initiatives as constructive to addressing issues of mutual interest and benefit for all three countries. Some critics of the most recent summit contend that the agenda did not include human rights issues or discussions on the drug-related violence in Mexico.

During the February 2014 Summit, President Obama, Mexican President Peña Nieto, and Canadian Prime Minister Stephen Harper announced initiatives regarding the economic prosperity of the region; education initiatives; energy and climate change; citizen security; and regional, global, and stakeholder outreach.[18] The leaders discussed numerous economic and security initiatives for North America in the 21st century with the goal of setting new global standards for trade, education, sustainable growth, and innovation. In the areas of economic cooperation, discussions included developing a North American Transportation Plan; streamlining procedures and harmonizing customs data requirements; facilitating the movement of people through the establishment in 2014 of a North American Trusted Traveler Program, which will recognize and build upon existing programs; promoting trilateral exchanges on logistics corridors and regional development; and continuing prior initiatives such as protecting and enforcing intellectual property rights. In energy cooperation, the leaders continued their commitment to developing and securing affordable, clean and reliable energy supplies to help drive economic growth and support sustainable development. The leaders committed to continuing cooperation on climate change and environmental cooperation; security; and effective information exchanges and coordination among law-enforcement authorities to counter drug trafficking, arms trafficking, money laundering, and other illicit activities. The three governments also stated that they share a commitment to combating human trafficking in all its forms and agreed to work toward improving services for the victims of this crime.[19]

Most efforts to increase cooperation, either through trilateral or bilateral endeavors, generally have followed the recommendations of special working groups created after the first North American Leaders' Summit in 2005. These recommendations included (1) increasing the competitiveness of North American businesses and economies through more compatible regulations; (2) making borders smarter and more secure by coordinating long-term infrastructure plans, enhancing services, and reducing bottlenecks and congestion at major border crossings; (3) strengthening energy security and protecting the environment by developing a framework for harmonization of energy efficiency standards and sharing technical information; (4) improving access to safe food and health and consumer products by increasing cooperation and information sharing on the safety of food and products; and (5) improving the North American response to

---

[18] The White House, Office of the Press Secretary, *Fact Sheet: Key Deliverables for the 2014 North American Leaders Summit,* February 19, 2014.

[19] The White House, Office of the Press Secretary, "Joint Statement by North American Leaders— 21st Century North America: Building the Most Competitive and Dynamic Region in the World," February 19, 2014.

emergencies by updating bilateral agreements to enable government authorities from the three countries to help each other more quickly and efficiently during times of crisis.

The Obama Administration has engaged in bilateral efforts, both with Canada and Mexico, to increase regulatory cooperation, enhance border security, promote economic competitiveness, and pursue energy integration. On September 20, 2013, the United States and Mexico launched the U.S.-Mexico High Level Economic Dialogue (HLED) to advance economic and commercial priorities through annual meetings at the cabinet level that also include leaders from the public and private sectors.[20] Other bilateral efforts with Mexico include the High-Level Regulatory Cooperation Council (HLRCC) launched in February 2012 to help align regulatory principles, an effort similar to the U.S.-Canada Regulatory Cooperation Council. In addition, the two countries have a bilateral initiative for border management under the Declaration Concerning Twenty-first Center Border Management that was announced in 2010.

The Mexican Economy

After increasing by an average of 3.8% in 2011-12, the growth rate of Mexico's gross domestic product (GDP) fell to 1.3% in 2013. GDP is forecast to grow by 2.4% in 2014. However, there is a chance that the economy will not reach its growth potential if consumer confidence does not pick up.[21] In the longer term, GDP growth could increase by an additional 1-2% if the government succeeds in implementing the structural reforms enacted through constitutional reforms in 2013, particularly the energy reforms approved in December 2013. This depends largely on whether the secondary legislation to implement those reforms is approved by the Mexican Congress and what the legislation entails. Mexico's economic growth has been limited by a need for structural reforms in the labor, education, energy, and fiscal sectors.

The Mexican government's policy efforts to stimulate the economy are expected to help economic growth in 2014. The central bank has cut interest rates, while the government has obtained congressional approval to widen the fiscal deficit in order to increase spending and increase economic growth.[22] In addition, the expected improvement in the U.S. economy is predicted to have a positive effect on Mexico's economy.[23] Trends in Mexico's GDP growth generally follow U.S. economic trends, as shown in **Figure 2**. The economy recovered in 2010 after a sharp contraction following the global financial crisis and subsequent downturn in the U.S. economy. GDP is estimated to have contracted by over 4.5% in 2009, while the Mexican peso depreciated against the dollar by 25%.[24] Mexico experienced the deepest recession in the Latin America region following the crisis. This is largely due to its high dependence on manufacturing exports to the United States, though other factors have also contributed. In the years that followed, Mexico's sound macroeconomic fundamentals, solid banking sector, and competitive export sector helped the economy and its ability to weather external conditions.

---

[20] The White House, Office of the Press Secretary, "Fact Sheet: U.S.-Mexico High Level Economic Dialogue," September 20, 2013.

[21] Economist Intelligence Unit (EIU), *Country Report: Mexico,* Generated on June 20, 2014.

[22] IHS Global Insight: Country and Industry Forecasting, *Country Outlook: Mexico,* updated on April 24, 2014.

[23] Ibid.

[24] International Monetary Fund (IMF), "IMF Executive Board Concludes 2010 Article IV Consultation with Mexico," Public Information Notice (PIN) No. 10/39, March 16, 2010, p. 2.

Figure 2. GDP Growth Rates for the United States and Mexico

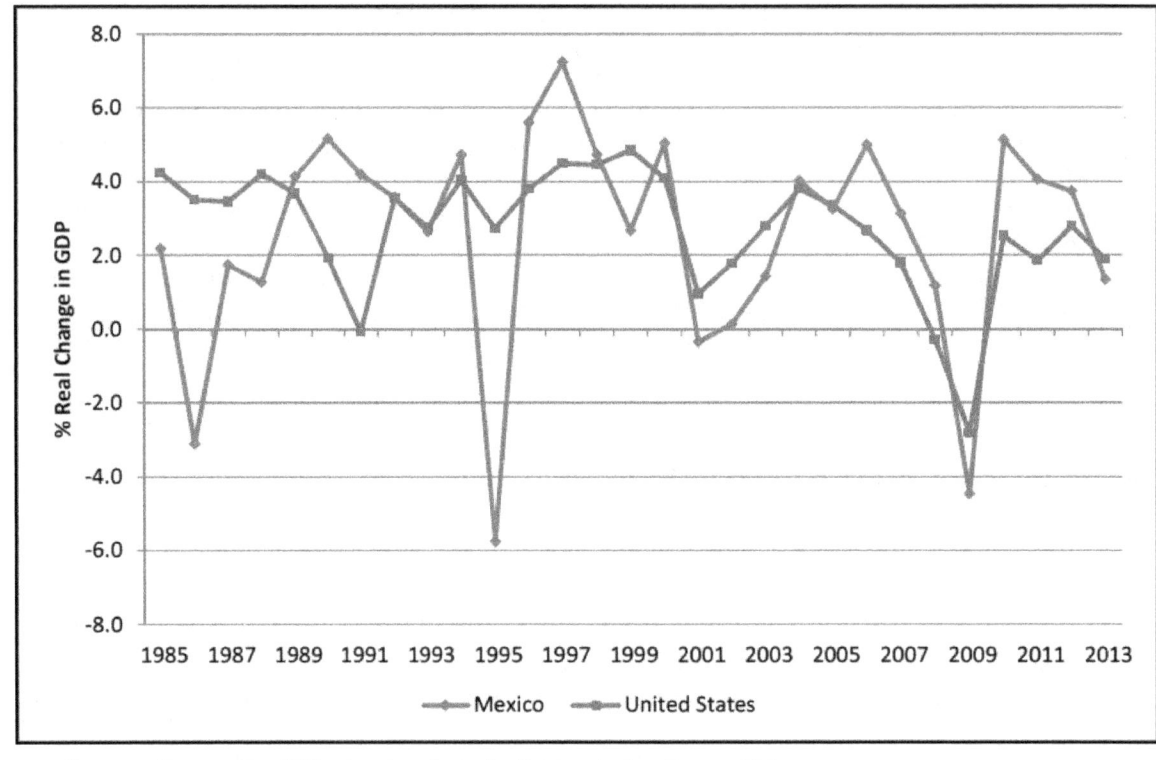

Source: Prepared by CRS using data from the Economist Intelligence Unit.

Informality and Poverty

Mexico has a large informal sector that is estimated to account for a considerable portion of total employment. Estimates on the size of the informal labor sector vary widely. One source estimates that the informal sector accounts for one-quarter to one-third of total employment[25], while another estimates that formal employment in Mexico only accounts for one-third of the labor force, which would indicate that two-thirds of the workforce is employed in the informal sector.[26] Under Mexico's legal framework, workers in the formal sector are defined as salaried workers employed by a firm that registers them with the government and are covered by Mexico's social security programs. Informal sector workers are defined as non-salaried workers who are usually self-employed. These workers have various degrees of entitlement to other social protection programs.[27] Salaried workers can be employed by industry, such as construction, agriculture, or services. Non-salaried employees are defined by exclusion and can be defined by various

---

[25] Gordon H. Hanson, *Understanding Mexico's Economic Underperformance*, the Woodrow Wilson International Center for Scholars and the Migration Policy Institute, August 2012, p. 6.

[26] IHS Global Insight: Country and Industry Forecasting, *Mexico: Country Outlook; Labor Markets*, updated on February 21, 2014.

[27] Santiago Levy, *Good Intentions, Bad Outcomes, Social Policy, Informality, and Economic Growth in Mexico*, Brookings Institution, 2008.

categories. These workers may include agricultural producers; seamstresses and tailors; artisans; street vendors; individuals who wash cars on the street; and other professions.[28]

Many workers in the informal sector suffer from poverty, which has been one of Mexico's more serious and pressing economic problems for many years. Although the government has made progress in poverty reduction efforts, poverty continues to be a basic challenge for the country's development. The Mexican government's main program from which many informal sector workers benefit is the conditional cash transfer program call *Oportunidades* (formerly known as Progresa). The program seeks to not only alleviate the immediate effects of poverty through cash and in-kind transfers, but to break the cycle of poverty by improving nutrition and health standards among poor families and increasing educational attainment. This program provides cash transfers to families in poverty who demonstrate that they regularly attend medical appointments and can certify that children are attending school. The government provides educational cash transfers to participating families. The program also provides nutrition support to pregnant and nursing women and malnourished children.[29]

Some economists and other experts cite the informal sector as a hindrance to the country's economic development. A 2012 report by the Migration Policy Institute contends that there are two lines of argument that attempt to explain the reason for such a large informal sector: (1) overregulation of businesses; and (2) an unintended incentive to informality created by Mexico's social protection programs.[30] The report cites evidence suggesting that the scale of informality in Mexico may result in a lower level of productivity, but it is not clear whether it hinders economic growth.[31] Another study published by the Brookings Institution presented a hypothesis that Mexico's social programs benefitting the informal sector have led to larger than optimal informal employment that has lowered aggregate labor productivity and caused a lower rate of growth in GDP.[32]

Structural and Other Economic Challenges

Numerous political analysts and economists agree that Mexico needs significant political and economic structural reforms to improve its potential for long-term economic growth. After the 1995 currency crisis, the Mexican government implemented numerous reform measures that helped the country modify its macroeconomic policies and restore policy credibility. Key reforms included measures to reduce public debt, the introduction of a balanced budget rule, an inflation targeting framework and a floating exchange rate policy.[33] Such policies positioned the country well in terms of macroeconomic and financial performance, but economic growth remains insufficient and many experts agree that more needs to be done to improve well-being in all regions of the country. A 2013 study by the Organization for Economic Cooperation and Development (OECD) states that the Mexican government must implement structural reforms

---

[28] Ibid, p. 12.

[29] For more information, see the Mexican government website: Secretaría de Desarrollo Social, *Oportunidades*, at http://www.oportunidades.gob mx.

[30] Gordon H. Hanson, p. 6.

[31] Ibid., p. 7.

[32] Santiago Levy, *Progress Against Poverty*, Brookings Institution, 2006.

[33] "Mexico Recovering, but Crisis Spotlights Challenges, says IMF," *IMF Survey Magazine: In the News*, March 16, 2010.

across multiple institutional domains to raise long-term economic growth.[34] The study states that the government should follow through on already-legislated reforms, notably in the key areas of labor markets, competition, and education to increase productivity. In addition, the study states that Mexico should consider new legislation and regulatory reform to remove barriers to market entry, reduce corruption, and make the civil justice system more effective.[35]

According to a 2014 study by the McKinsey Global Institute, Mexico has been successful in creating certain sectors of the economy that are highly competitive in the world market, but has not been so successful in others.[36] The study describes a "dualistic" nature of the Mexican economy in which there is a modern Mexico with sophisticated automotive and aerospace factories, multinationals that compete in global markets, and universities that graduate high numbers of engineers. In contrast, the other part of Mexico, according to the study, is technologically backward, unproductive, and operates outside the formal economy.[37] The study states that three decades of economic reforms have failed to raise the overall GDP growth. Government measures to privatize industries, liberalize trade, and welcome foreign investment have created a side to the economy that is highly productive in which numerous industries have flourished, but the reforms have not been successful in touching other sectors of the economy where traditional enterprises have not modernized, informality is rising, and productivity is plunging.[38]

A key challenge to increasing productivity is the issue of monopolies and limited competition. A 2009 book co-published by the World Bank and Palgrave Macmillan,[39] as well as numerous reports and journal articles, report that special interest groups have blocked changes in Mexico that would introduce more market forces into the economy. The publication states that "Mexico seems to be caught up in a high-inequality, low growth state" and that reforms must be put into place in order for Mexico to improve economic growth.[40] A key issue discussed is the oil industry, which, according to the book, is controlled by the government and the oil industry labor union. The book argues that the certain interest groups, including the government, energy-intensive industrial firms, and the industry's labor union, have prevented change from taking place in the oil sector because change would eliminate many of the benefits they have received for many years.[41] Pemex's labor union is concerned that thousands of jobs are likely to be at stake as the company is opened up to competition. The large industrial companies that use large amounts of energy at subsidized prices do not want to lose these benefits under a more competitive environment.[42] They could potentially benefit, however, if Pemex reform and the opening of new gas pipelines from the United States lowers energy costs (including electricity costs) for companies and consumers. They could also benefit from increased foreign investment, which would likely enhance competitiveness and lead to further growth.

---

[34] Organization for Economic Cooperation and Development (OECD), *OECD Economic Surveys— Mexico*, May 2013.

[35] Ibid.

[36] Eduardo Bolio, Jaana Remes, and Tomas Lajous, et al., *A tale of two Mexicos: Growth and Prosperity in a Two-Speed Economy*, McKinsey Global Institute, March 2014.

[37] Ibid.

[38] Ibid., p. 2.

[39] Levy, Santiago, and Michael Walton, editors, *No Growth Without Equity?— Inequality, Interests, and Competition in Mexico*, (Washington, DC: Palgrave MacMillan and The World Bank, 2009).

[40] Ibid, p. 417.

[41] Ibid.

[42] Elisabeth Malkin, "Are Monopolies Holding Mexico Back," *The New York Times*, June 2, 2009.

Energy Sector

Mexico's long-term economic outlook depends largely on the energy sector. Mexico is one of the 10 largest oil producers in the world, and is the third-largest in the Western Hemisphere. However, Mexico's oil production has steadily decreased since 2005 as a result of natural production declines. [43] The oil sector generated 13% of Mexico's export earnings in 2013. [44] The Mexican government depends heavily on oil revenues, which provide 30% to 40% of the government's fiscal revenues. Many industry experts contend that Mexican oil production has peaked, and that the country's production will continue to decline in the coming years unless the Mexican government reforms its energy sector. The Mexican government has used oil revenues from its state oil company, Pemex, for government operating expenses, which has come at the expense of needed reinvestment in the company itself. In the final quarter of 2013, Pemex reportedly paid 50% of its revenue ($16 billion) in taxes to the federal government yet posted a total loss of $13 billion for 2013. [45] Because the government relies so heavily on oil income, any decline in revenue has major fiscal implications.

According to industry exports, Mexico has the potential resources to support a long-term recovery in total production, primarily in the Gulf of Mexico. [46] However, the country does not have the technical capability or financial means to develop potential deepwater projects or shale oil deposits in the north. Mexico's oil and natural gas production is unlikely to increase without improvement in Pemex's financial situation, technical abilities, and terms for investors. [47]

In December 2013, President Peña Nieto signed into law constitutional reforms related to Mexico's energy sector that aim to bolster the country's declining oil production and to allow private and foreign investment to help Pemex tap into the country's shale and deep water reserves. [48] Emilio Lozoya, the head of Pemex, has predicted that the secondary laws could boost FDI in Mexico to $50 to $60 billion per year. [49] The legal framework for the reforms must be approved by the Mexican Congress before the changes take place. The first round of contracts is expected to take place six months after the legislation is approved. [50] The energy reform is the centerpiece of the Peña Nieto administration's attempts to overhaul the economy, attract greater foreign investment and generate more jobs. [51] While most experts predict that the Mexican Congress will approve the secondary legislation, the future shape of relations between the government, or Pemex, and private oil companies will likely be a work in progress as the sector adapts to the new legal system. [52] Foreign observers expect the secondary legislation to become law in July 2014. [53]

---

[43] U.S. Energy Information Administration (EIA), *Country Analysis Briefs: Mexico*, April 24, 2014.

[44] Ibid.

[45] Adam Williams, "Mexico's Oil May Offer Gusher for Foreigners," *The Washington Post*, June 8, 2014, p. G3.

[46] EIA, April 24, 2014.

[47] Ibid.

[48] For more information, CRS Report R43313, *Mexico's Oil and Gas Sector: Background, Reform Efforts, and Implications for the United States*, coordinated by Clare Ribando Seelke.

[49] Valerie Volcovici, "Pemex Chief Touts Mexico's Energy Reform in Washington Visit," *Reuters*, April 24, 2014.

[50] Jude Webber, "Mexico to Unveil Oil Tender Process," *Financial Times*, June 17, 2014.

[51] EIU, "Debate on Key Energy Bylaws Gets Underway," June 12, 2014.

[52] Ibid.

[53] Diana Villiers Negroponte, *Mexico's Secondary Law Provides a Path Forward for New Investments in the* (continued...)

While it is difficult to predict how increasing private participation in Mexico's oil and gas sectors would affect the country's economic development, skeptics see reason to doubt the government's positive predictions. Some argue that multinational companies and large Mexican conglomerates stand more to gain from the energy reform than the Mexican people.[54] Other critics question the government's claim that the reforms will create thousands of jobs and maintain that because Pemex is a bloated company with too many employees, it would likely shed workers as a result of the reform. Others are concerned that the oil revenue will be mishandled by corrupt Pemex or government officials rather than invested in strategic ways that will benefit the country as a whole.[55]

Mexico's leftist PRD party firmly opposes the reform, arguing that the reforms do not include measures to address corruption, transparency, government accountability, worker rights, and protection of affected communities and land owner rights.[56] It has called for a *consulta popular*, or referendum, on the acceptance on whether the acceptance or rejection of the energy reform is constitutionally permissible.

In February 2012, the United States and Mexico signed the U.S.-Mexico Trans-Boundary Hydrocarbon agreement, which addresses issues related to the development of oil and gas reservoirs that cross the international maritime boundary between the two countries in the Gulf of Mexico. After review by the U.S. Congress, the agreement was approved as part of the Bipartisan Budget Act of 2013 (P.L. 113-67).[57] The agreement clarifies U.S. interests in an estimated 172 million barrels of oil and 304 billion cubic feet of natural gas. According to the U.S. Department of the Interior, the agreement involves two U.S. actions: lifting a moratorium and jointly developing resources in a "transboundary area"— areas straddling the U.S.-Mexico marine border.[58] The Obama Administration views the agreement as a step forward in clarifying relations between the two countries in managing energy resources in portions of the Gulf of Mexico and also represents an example of U.S.-Mexico efforts to develop a sustainable energy trade relationship.[59]

Mexico's Regional Free Trade Agreements

Mexico has had a growing commitment to trade integration and liberalization through the formation of free trade agreements (FTAs) since the 1990s, and its trade policy is among the most open in the world. The pursuit of FTAs with other countries not only provides economic benefits, but could also potentially reduce Mexico's economic dependence on the United States. In an

---

(...continued)

Hydrocarbons Sector, Brookings, June 25, 2014.

[54] "Richard Fausset, "Tons of Thousands Protest Mexican Oil Reforms," *Los Angeles Times*, September 8, 2013.

[55] Enrique Krauze, "Mexico's Theology of Oil," *New York Times*, November 1, 2013.

[56] Party of the Democratic Revolution (*Partido de la Revolución Democrática;* PRD), "National Position of the PRD and its Parliamentary Groups in the Senate and the Chamber of Deputies regarding the Secondary Legislation on Energy Matters," June 10, 2014.

[57] See CRS Report R43606, *U.S.-Mexico Transboundary Hydrocarbons Agreement: Background and Issues for Congress*, by Curry L. Hagerty.

[58] CRS Report, CRS Report R43606, *U.S.-Mexico Transboundary Hydrocarbons Agreement: Background and Issues for Congress*, by Curry L. Hagerty, pp. 1-2.

[59] U.S. Department of State, "Remarks by Secretary of State Hillary Rodham Clinton at the Signing of the U.S.-Mexico Transboundary Agreement," February 20, 2012.

effort to increase trade with other countries, Mexico has a total of 12 free trade agreements involving 44 countries. These include agreements with most countries in the Western Hemisphere, including the United States and Canada under NAFTA, Chile, Colombia, Costa Rica, Nicaragua, Peru, Guatemala, El Salvador, and Honduras.

Mexico has ventured out of the hemisphere in negotiating FTAs, and, in July 2000, entered into agreements with Israel and the European Union. Mexico became the first Latin American country to have preferred access to these two markets. Mexico has also completed an FTA with the European Free Trade Association (EFTA) of Iceland, Liechtenstein, Norway, and Switzerland. The Mexican government has continued to look for potential free trade partners, and expanded its outreach to Asia in 2000 by entering into negotiations with Singapore, Korea, and Japan. Negotiations on FTAs with Korea and Singapore are stalled. In addition to the bilateral and multilateral free trade agreements, Mexico is a member of the WTO,[60] the Asia-Pacific Economic Cooperation (APEC) forum, and the OECD.

Proposed Trans-Pacific Partnership (TPP) Agreement

The TPP is a proposed regional FTA being negotiated among the United States, Australia, Brunei, Canada, Chile, Japan, Malaysia, Mexico, New Zealand, Peru, Singapore, and Vietnam.[61] On June 18, 2012, President Obama announced that the countries involved in the negotiations at the time had extended an invitation to Mexico and Canada to join negotiations for the proposed regional trade agreement. With the start of the Auckland Round in December 2012, Mexico and Canada began participating in the TPP negotiations. U.S. negotiators and others describe and envision the TPP as a "comprehensive and high-standard" FTA that aims to liberalize trade in nearly all goods and services. If negotiations are concluded, the agreement would likely include commitments that go beyond NAFTA and those currently established in the World Trade Organization (WTO). The proposed TPP potentially could eliminate tariff and non-tariff barriers to trade and investment among member countries and could serve as a template for a future trade pact with other countries. Twenty-nine chapters are currently under discussion. In addition to market access, negotiations are being conducted on disciplines regarding protection of intellectual property rights, trade in services, government procurement, foreign investment, rules of origin, labor, and environmental standards.

The proposed TPP would likely enhance the links Mexico already has with the United States and Canada under NAFTA. The Mexican government agreed to several conditions that TPP countries had placed on its entry into the negotiations, including a commitment to "high standards." The conditions included that Mexico would not be able to reopen any existing agreements that were

---

[60] The WTO allows member countries to form regional trade agreements under Article under certain rules. The position of the WTO is that regional trade agreements can often support the WTO's multilateral trading system by allowing groups of countries to negotiate rules and commitments that go beyond what was possible at the time under the WTO. The WTO has a committee on regional trade agreements that examines regional groups and assesses whether they are consistent with WTO rules. See The World Trade Organization, "Understanding the WTO: Cross-Cutting and New Issues, Regionalism: Friends or Rivals?" http://www.wto.org.

[61] For more information, see CRS Report R42694, *The Trans-Pacific Partnership (TPP) Negotiations and Issues for Congress*, coordinated by Ian F. Fergusson, and CRS Report R42344, *Trans-Pacific Partnership (TPP) Countries: Comparative Trade and Economic Analysis*, by Brock R. Williams.

already made by the current TPP partners, unless they agreed to revisit something previously agreed upon.

NAFTA

The North American Free Trade Agreement (NAFTA) has been in effect since January 1994.[62] The overall economic impact of NAFTA is difficult to measure since trade and investment trends are influenced by numerous other economic variables such as economic growth, inflation, and currency fluctuations. The agreement may have accelerated the trade liberalization that was already taking place between the United States and Mexico, but many of these changes may have taken place with or without an agreement. Nevertheless, NAFTA is significant because it was the most comprehensive free trade agreement (FTA) negotiated at the time, and contained several groundbreaking provisions. There are numerous indications that NAFTA has achieved many of the intended trade and economic benefits, as well as incurred adjustment costs. This has been in keeping with what most economists maintain, that trade liberalization promotes overall economic growth among trading partners, but that there are significant adjustment costs.

Most of the trade effects in the United States related to NAFTA are due to changes in U.S. trade and investment patterns with Mexico. At the time of NAFTA implementation, the U.S.-Canada Free Trade Agreement already had been in effect for five years, and some industries in the United States and Canada were already highly integrated. Mexico, on the other hand, had followed an aggressive import-substitution policy for many years prior to NAFTA in which it had sought to develop certain domestic industries through trade protection. One example is the Mexican automotive industry, which had been regulated by a series of five decrees issued by the Mexican government between 1962 and 1989. The decrees established import tariffs as high as 25% on automotive goods and had high restrictions on foreign auto production in Mexico. Under NAFTA, Mexico agreed to eliminate these restrictive trade policies.

Prior to NAFTA, Mexico was already liberalizing its protectionist trade and investment policies that had been in place for decades. The restrictive trade regime began after Mexico's revolutionary period, and remained until the early to mid-1980s, when it began to shift to a more open, export-oriented economy. For Mexico, an FTA with the United States represented a way to lock in the trade reforms, attract greater flows of foreign investment, and spur economic growth. For the United States, NAFTA represented an opportunity to expand the growing export market to the south, but it also represented a political opportunity to improve the relationship with Mexico.

Estimating the economic impact of trade agreements is very difficult due to a lack of data and important theoretical and practical matters associated with generating results from economic models. In addition, such estimates provide an incomplete accounting of the total economic effects of trade agreements.[63] Numerous studies suggest that NAFTA achieved many of the intended trade and economic benefits.[64] Other studies suggest that NAFTA has come at a cost to

---

[62] For more information on NAFTA, see CRS Report R42965, *NAFTA at 20: Overview and Trade Effects*, by M. Angeles Villarreal and Ian F. Fergusson.

[63] For more information, see CRS Report R41660, *U.S.-South Korea Free Trade Agreement and Potential Employment Effects: Analysis of Studies*, by Mary Jane Bolle and James K. Jackson.

[64] See, for example, Gary Clyde Hufbauer and Jeffrey J. Schott, *NAFTA Revisited: Achievements and Challenges*, Institute for International Economics, October 2005; Center for Strategic and International Studies, *NAFTA's Impact on North America: The First Decade*, Edited by Sidney Weintraub, 2004; and U.S. Chamber of Commerce, *Opening* (continued...)

U.S. workers.[65] This has been in keeping with what most economists maintain, that trade liberalization promotes overall economic growth among trading partners, but that there are both winners and losers from adjustments.

Not all changes in trade and investment patterns within North America since 1994 can be attributed to NAFTA because trade has also been affected by a number of factors. The sharp devaluation of the peso at the end of the 1990s and the associated recession in Mexico had considerable effects on trade, as did the rapid growth of the U.S. economy during most of the 1990s and, more recently, the economic slowdown caused by the 2008 financial crisis. Trade-related job gains and losses since NAFTA may have accelerated trends that were ongoing prior to NAFTA and may not be totally attributable to the trade agreement.

Many economists and other observers have credited NAFTA with helping U.S. manufacturing industries, especially the U.S. auto industry, become more globally competitive through the development of supply chains.[66] Much of the increase in U.S.-Mexico trade, for example, can be attributed to specialization as manufacturing and assembly plants have reoriented to take advantage of economies of scale. As a result, supply chains have been increasingly crossing national boundaries as manufacturing work is performed wherever it is most efficient.[67] A reduction in tariffs in a given sector not only affects prices in that sector but also in industries that purchase intermediate inputs from that sector. The expansion of trade resulted in the creation of vertical supply relationships, especially along the U.S.-Mexico border. The flow of intermediate inputs produced in the United States and exported to Mexico and the return flow of finished products greatly increased the importance of the U.S.-Mexico border region as a production site. U.S. manufacturing industries, including automotive, electronics, appliances, and machinery, all rely on the assistance of Mexican manufacturers. One study estimates that 40% of the content of U.S. imports from Mexico and 25% of the content of U.S. imports from Canada are of U.S. origin. In comparison, U.S. imports from China are said to have only 4% U.S. content. Taken together, goods from Mexico and Canada represent about 75% of all the U.S. domestic content that returns to the United States as imports.[68]

Bilateral Trade Issues

Sugar Disputes

On March 28, 2014, the American Sugar Coalition and its members filed a petition with the U.S. International Trade Commission (ITC) and the Department of Commerce (DOC) alleging that

---

(...continued)

Markets, Creating Jobs: Estimated U.S. Employment Effects of Trade with FTA Partners, 2010.

[65] See, for example, Robert E. Scott, *Heading South: U.S.-Mexico Trade and Job Displacement under NAFTA*, Economic Policy Institute, May 3, 2011; and the Frederick S. Pardee Center, *The Future of North American Trade Policy: Lessons from NAFTA*, Boston University, November 2009.

[66] Hufbauer and Schott, *NAFTA Revisited*, pp. 20-21.

[67] Ibid., p. 21.

[68] Robert Koopman, William Powers, and Zhi Wang, et al., *Giver Credit Where Credit is Due: Tracing Value Added in Global Production Chains*, National Bureau of Economic Research, Working Paper 16426, Cambridge, MA, September 2010, pp. 7-8.

Mexico was dumping and subsidizing its sugar exports to the United States. Sugar producers are claiming that Mexico's actions will cost the industry $1 billion in 2014. On April 18, 2014, the DOC announced the initiation of antidumping duty and countervailing duty investigations of sugar imports from Mexico.[69] On May 9, 2014, the U.S. International Trade Commission issued a preliminary report stating that there is a "reasonable indication that an industry in the United States is materially injured by reason of imports of sugar from Mexico that are allegedly sold in the United States at less than fair value and allegedly subsidized by the Government of Mexico."[70] Final rulings by the Department of Commerce and the ITC may not occur until 2015.

In 2006, the United States and Mexico resolved another trade dispute involving sugar and high fructose corn syrup. The dispute involved a sugar side letter negotiated under NAFTA. Mexico argued that the side letter entitled it to ship net sugar surplus to the United States duty-free under NAFTA, while the United States argued that the sugar side letter limited Mexican shipments of sugar. In addition, Mexico complained that imports of high fructose corn syrup (HFCS) sweeteners from the United States constituted dumping. It imposed anti-dumping duties for some time, until NAFTA and WTO dispute resolution panels upheld U.S. claims that the Mexican government colluded with the Mexican sugar and sweetener industries to restrict HFCS imports from the United States.

In late 2001, the Mexican Congress imposed a 20% tax on soft drinks made with corn syrup sweeteners to aid the ailing domestic cane sugar industry, and subsequently extended the tax annually despite U.S. objections. In 2004, the United States Trade Representative (USTR) initiated WTO dispute settlement proceedings against Mexico's HFCS tax, and following interim decisions, the WTO panel issued a final decision on October 7, 2005, essentially supporting the U.S. position. Mexico appealed this decision, and in March 2006, the WTO Appellate Body upheld its October 2005 ruling. In July 2006, the United States and Mexico agreed that Mexico would eliminate its tax on soft drinks made with corn sweeteners no later than January 31, 2007. The tax was repealed, effective January 1, 2007.

The United States and Mexico reached a sweetener agreement in August 2006. Under the agreement, Mexico can export 500,000 metric tons of sugar duty-free to the United States from October 1, 2006, to December 31, 2007. The United States can export the same amount of HFCS duty-free to Mexico during that time. NAFTA provides for the free trade of sweeteners beginning January 1, 2008. The House and Senate sugar caucuses expressed objections to the agreement, questioning the Bush Administration's determination that Mexico is a net-surplus sugar producer to allow Mexican sugar duty-free access to the U.S. market.[71]

---

[69] For more information, see International Trade Administration, *Fact Sheet: Commerce Initiates Antidumping Duty and Countervailing Duty Investigations of Imports of Sugar from Mexico,* at http://enforcement.trade.gov/download/factsheets/factsheet-mexico-sugar-cvd-initiation-041814.pdf.

[70] U.S. International Trade Commission, *Sugar from Mexico, Investigation Nos. 701-TA-513 and 731-TA-1249 (Preliminary)*, Publication 4467, Washington, DC, May 2014, p. 3.

[71] See "Bush Administration Defends Sugar Deal to Congress," *Inside U.S. Trade,* November 3, 2006; "Grassley, U.S. Industry Welcome Agreement with Mexico on Sugar, HFCS," *International Trade Reporter,* August 3, 2006; and, "U.S., Mexico Reach Agreement on WTO Soft Drink Dispute Compliance Deadline," *International Trade Reporter,* July 13, 2006.

Mexican Tomatoes

In February 2013, the United States and Mexico reached a tentative agreement on cross-border trade in tomatoes, averting a potential trade war between the two countries.[72] On March 4, 2013, the Department of Commerce (DOC) and the government of Mexico officially signed the agreement suspending the antidumping investigation on fresh tomatoes from Mexico.[73] The dispute began on June 22, 2012, when a group of Florida tomato growers, who were backed by growers in other states, asked the DOC and the U.S. International Trade Commission to terminate an antidumping duty suspension pact on tomatoes from Mexico. The termination of the pact, which sets a minimum reference price for Mexican tomatoes in the United States, would have effectively led to an antidumping investigation on Mexican tomatoes. Mexico's Ambassador to the United States at the time, Arturo Sarukhan, warned that such an action would damage the U.S.-Mexico trade agenda and bilateral trade relationship as a whole. He also stated that Mexico would use all resources at its disposal, including the possibility of retaliatory tariffs, to defend the interests of the Mexican tomato industry.[74] The Florida Tomato Exchange, a coalition of Florida tomato growers, is challenging the suspension agreement and has a pending lawsuit filed with the U.S. Court of International Trade.[75]

The suspension pact dates back to 1996, when the DOC, under pressure from Florida tomato growers, filed an anti-dumping petition against Mexican tomato growers and began an investigation into whether they were dumping Mexican tomatoes on the U.S. market at below-market prices. NAFTA, which entered into force in January 1994, had eliminated U.S. tariffs on Mexican tomatoes, causing an inflow of fresh tomatoes from Mexico. Florida tomato growers complained that Mexican tomato growers were selling tomatoes at below-market prices. After the 1996 filing of the petition, the DOC and Mexican producers and exporters of tomatoes reached an agreement under which Mexican tomato growers agreed to revise their prices by setting a minimum reference price in order to eliminate the injurious effects of fresh tomato exports to the United States.[76] The so-called "suspension agreement" remained in place for years and was renewed in 2002 and 2008.[77]

The 2013 suspension agreement covers all fresh and chilled tomatoes, excluding those intended for use in processing. It increases the number of tomato categories with established reference prices from one to four. It also raises reference prices at which tomatoes can be sold in the U.S. market to better reflect the changes in the marketplace since the last agreement had been signed. It continues to account for winter and summer seasons.[78]

---

[72] Stephanie Strom, "United States and Mexico Reach Tomato Deal, Averting a Trade War," *New York Times*, February 4, 2013.

[73] U.S. Department of Commerce, Import Administration, *Fresh Tomatoes from Mexico 1996 Suspension Agreement*, available at http://ia.ita.doc.gov/tomato/index html.

[74] Rosella Brevetti, "Mexico Ambassador Warns Against ending U.S. Suspension Agreement on Tomatoes," *International Trade Reporter*, September 20, 2012.

[75] Brian Flood, "Florida Tomato Trade Group Loses Bid to Block Evidence in Mexico Dispute," *Bloomberg BNA*, April 15, 2014.

[76] U.S. Department of Commerce, Import Administration, *Fresh Tomatoes from Mexico 1996 Suspension Agreement*, available at http://ia.ita.doc.gov/tomato/index html.

[77] Ibid.

[78] Len Bracken, "Commerce, Mexican Tomato Growers Agree on Final Version of Antidumping Agreement," *International Trade Daily*, March 5, 2013.

When they filed the 2012 petition asking for the termination of the suspension agreement, U.S. tomato producers argued that the pacts had not worked. The petitioners stated that it was necessary to end the agreement with Mexico in order to "restore fair competition to the market and eliminate the predatory actions of producers in Mexico."[79] However, business groups urged the DOC to proceed cautiously in the tomato dispute since termination could result in higher tomato prices in the United States and lead Mexico to implement retaliatory measures. Some businesses urged a continuation of the agreement, arguing that it helped stabilize the market and provide U.S. consumers with consistent and predictable pricing. According to a *New York Times* article, the Mexican tomato producers enlisted roughly 370 U.S. businesses, including Wal-Mart Stores and meat and vegetable producers, to argue their cause.[80]

Dolphin-Safe Tuna Labeling Dispute

The United States and Mexico are involved in a trade dispute regarding U.S. dolphin-safe labeling provisions and tuna imports from Mexico. U.S. labeling provisions establish conditions under which tuna products may voluntarily be labeled as "dolphin-safe." These products may not be labeled as dolphin-safe if the tuna is caught by intentionally encircling dolphins with nets. According to the Office of the United States Trade Representative (USTR), some Mexican fishing vessels use this method when fishing for tuna. Mexico asserts that U.S. tuna labeling provisions deny Mexican tuna effective access to the U.S. market.[81]

In October 2008, Mexico filed a request for World Trade Organization (WTO) dispute settlement consultations with the United States regarding U.S. provisions on voluntary dolphin-safe labeling on tuna products. The United States requested that Mexico refrain from proceeding in the WTO and that the case be moved to the NAFTA dispute resolution mechanism. According to the USTR, however, Mexico "blocked that process for settling this dispute."[82] In September 2011, a WTO panel determined that the objectives of U.S. voluntary tuna labeling provisions were legitimate and that any adverse effects felt by Mexican tuna producers were the result of choices made by Mexico's own fishing fleet and canners. However, the panel also found U.S. labeling provisions to be "more restrictive than necessary to achieve the objectives of the measures."[83] The Obama Administration appealed the WTO ruling.

On May 16, 2012, the WTO's Appellate Body overturned two key findings from the September 2011 WTO dispute panel. The Appellate Body found that U.S. tuna labeling requirements violate global trade rules because they treat imported tuna from Mexico less favorably than U.S. tuna. The Appellate Body also rejected Mexico's claim that U.S. tuna labeling requirements were more trade-restrictive than necessary to meet the U.S. objective of minimizing dolphin deaths.[84] The United States had a deadline of July 13, 2013, to comply with the WTO dispute ruling. In July 2013, the United States issued a final rule amending certain dolphin-safe labelling requirements

---

[79] *Inside U.S. Trade's World Trade Online*, "U.S. Growers Seek to End Suspension Agreement on Mexican Tomato Imports," June 28, 2012.

[80] Stephanie Strom, *New York Times*, February 4, 2013.

[81] Office of the United States Trade Representative (USTR), "U.S. Appeal in WTO Dolphin-Safe Tuna Labeling Dispute with Mexico," January 23, 2012.

[82] Ibid.

[83] Ibid. For more information, see the USTR website at http://www.ustr.gov.

[84] Daniel Pruzin, "Appellate Body Overturns Key Panel Findings on U.S. Tuna-Dolphin Labeling Requirements," *International Trade Reporter*, May 24, 2012.

to bring it into compliance with the WTO labeling requirements. On November 14, 2013, Mexico requested the establishment of a WTO compliance panel. On April 16, 2014, the Chair of the compliance panel announced that it expects to issue its final report to the parties by December 2014.[85]

The government of Mexico had requested the United States to broaden its dolphin-safe rules to include Mexico's long-standing tuna fishing technique. It cited statistics showing that modern equipment has greatly reduced dolphin mortality from its height in the 1960s and that its ships carry independent observers who can verify dolphin safety.[86] However, some environmental groups that monitor the tuna industry disputed claims by the Mexican government, stating that even if no dolphins are killed during the chasing and netting, some are wounded and later die. In other cases, they argued, young dolphin calves may not be able to keep pace and are separated from their mothers and later die. These groups contended that if the United States changed its labeling requirements, cans of Mexican tuna could be labeled as "dolphin-safe" when it was not.[87] However, an industry spokesperson representing three major tuna processors in the United States, including StarKist, Bumblebee, and Chicken of the Sea, contended that U.S. companies would probably not buy Mexican tuna even if it is labeled as dolphin-safe because these companies "would not be in the market for tuna that is not caught in the dolphin-safe manner."[88]

The tuna labeling dispute began over 10 years ago. In April 2000, the Clinton Administration lifted an embargo on Mexican tuna under relaxed standards for a dolphin-safe label. This was in accordance with internationally agreed procedures and U.S. legislation passed in 1997 that encouraged the unharmed release of dolphins from nets. However, a federal judge in San Francisco ruled that the standards of the law had not been met, and the Federal Appeals Court in San Francisco sustained the ruling in July 2001. Under the Bush Administration, the Commerce Department ruled on December 31, 2002, that the dolphin-safe label may be applied if qualified observers certify that no dolphins were killed or seriously injured in the netting process. Environmental groups, however, filed a suit to block the modification. On April 10, 2003, the U.S. District Court for the Northern District of California enjoined the Commerce Department from modifying the standards for the dolphin-safe label. On August 9, 2004, the federal district court ruled against the Bush Administration's modification of the dolphin-safe standards and reinstated the original standards in the 1990 Dolphin Protection Consumer Information Act. That decision was appealed to the U.S. Ninth Circuit Court of Appeals, which ruled against the Administration in April 2007, finding that the Department of Commerce did not base its determination on scientific studies of the effects of Mexican tuna fishing on dolphins. In late October 2008, Mexico initiated World Trade Organization dispute proceedings against the United States, maintaining that U.S. requirements for Mexican tuna exporters prevents them from using the U.S. "dolphin-safe" label for its products.[89]

---

[85] For more information, see World Trade Organization, *United States— Measures Concerning the Importation, Marketing, and Sale of Tuna and Tuna Products,* available at http://www.wto.org.

[86] Tim Carman, "Tuna, meat labeling disputes highlight WTO control," *Washington Post,* January 10, 2012.

[87] Ibid.

[88] Ibid.

[89] Daniel Pruzin, "Mexico Initiates WTO Dispute Proceeding Against U.S. 'Dolphin-Safe' Label for Tuna," *International Trade Reporter*, October 30, 2008.

Mexican Trucking Issue

A major trade issue regarding NAFTA between the United States and Mexico for many years was the U.S. implementation of NAFTA trucking provisions. Under NAFTA, Mexican commercial trucks were to have been given full access to four U.S. border states in 1995 and full access throughout the United States in 2000. Citing safety concerns, however, the United States refused to implement NAFTA's trucking provisions. The Mexican government objected and claimed that U.S. actions were a violation of U.S. commitments under NAFTA. A NAFTA dispute resolution panel supported Mexico's position in February 2001. President Bush indicated a willingness to implement the provision, but the U.S. Congress required additional safety provisions in the FY2002 Department of Transportation Appropriations Act (P.L. 107-87). The United States and Mexico cooperated to resolve the issue and engaged in numerous talks regarding safety and operational issues. On July 6, 2011, the two countries signed a Memorandum of Understanding (MOU) to resolve the dispute. In October 2011, the United States granted the first permit to provide international long-haul cargo services to a Mexican trucking company. The pilot program is expected to conclude in October 2014.

Bush Administration's Pilot Program of 2007

On November 27, 2002, with safety inspectors and procedures in place, the Bush Administration announced that it would begin the process that would open U.S. highways to Mexican truckers and buses. However, environmental and labor groups went to court in early December to block the action. On January 16, 2003, the U.S. Court of Appeals for the Ninth Circuit ruled that full environmental impact statements were required for Mexican trucks to be allowed to operate on U.S. highways. The U.S. Supreme Court reversed that decision on June 7, 2004.

In February 2007, the Bush Administration announced a pilot project to grant Mexican trucks from 100 transportation companies full access to U.S. highways. In September 2007, the Department of Transportation (DOT) launched a one-year pilot program to allow approved Mexican carriers beyond the 25-mile commercial zone in the border region, with a similar program allowing U.S. trucks to travel beyond Mexico's border and commercial zone. Over the 18 months that the program existed, 29 motor carriers from Mexico were granted operating authority in the United States. Two of these carriers dropped out of the program shortly after being accepted, while two others never sent trucks across the border. In total, 103 Mexican trucks were used by the carriers as part of the program.[90]

In the FY2008 Consolidated Appropriations Act (P.L. 110-161), signed into law in December 2007, Congress included a provision prohibiting the use of FY2008 funding for the establishment of the pilot program. However, the DOT determined that it could continue with the pilot program because it had already been established. In March 2008, the DOT issued an interim report on the cross-border trucking demonstration project to the Senate Committee on Commerce, Science, and Transportation. The report made three key observations: (1) the Federal Motor Carrier Safety Administration (FMCSA) planned to check every participating truck each time it crossed the border to ensure that it met safety standards; (2) there was less participation in the project than

---

[90] Ibid.

was expected; and (3) the FMCSA implemented methods to assess possible adverse safety impacts of the project and to enforce and monitor safety guidelines.[91]

In early August 2008, DOT announced that it would be extending the pilot program for an additional two years. In opposition to this action, the House approved on September 9, 2008 (by a vote of 396 to 128), H.R. 6630, a bill that would have prohibited DOT from granting Mexican trucks access to U.S. highways beyond the border and commercial zone. The bill also would have prohibited DOT from renewing such a program unless expressly authorized by Congress. No action was taken by the Senate on the measure.

On March 11, 2009, the FY2009 Omnibus Appropriations Act (P.L. 111-8) terminated the pilot program. The FY2010 Consolidated Appropriations Act, passed in December 2009 (P.L. 111-117), did not preclude funds from being spent on a long-haul Mexican truck pilot program, provided that certain terms and conditions were satisfied. Numerous Members of Congress urged President Obama to find a resolution to the dispute in light of the effects that Mexico's retaliatory tariffs were having on U.S. producers (see section below).

A truck safety statistic on "out-of-service" rates indicates that Mexican trucks operating in the United States are now safer than they were a decade ago. The data indicate that Mexican trucks and drivers have a comparable safety record to U.S. truckers. Another study indicates that the truck driver is usually the more critical factor in causing accidents than a safety defect with the truck itself. Service characteristics of long-haul trucking suggest that substandard carriers would likely not succeed in this market.[92]

Mexico's Retaliatory Tariffs of 2009 and 2010

In response to the abrupt end of the pilot program, the Mexican government announced in March 2009 that it would retaliate by increasing duties on 90 U.S. products with a value of $2.4 billion in exports to Mexico. Mexico began imposing tariffs in March 2009 and, after reaching an understanding with the United States, eliminated them in two stages in 2011. The retaliatory tariffs, which went into effect on March 19, 2009, ranged from 10% to 45% and covered a range of products that included fruit, vegetables, home appliances, consumer products, and paper.[93] Subsequently, a group of 56 Members of the House of Representatives wrote to United States Trade Representative Ron Kirk and DOT Secretary Ray LaHood requesting the Administration to resolve the trucking issue.[94] The bipartisan group of Members stated that they wanted the issue to be resolved soon because the higher Mexican tariffs were having a "devastating" impact on local industries, especially in agriculture, and area economies in some states. One reported estimate stated that U.S. potato exports to Mexico had fallen 50% by value since the tariffs were imposed and that U.S. exporters were losing market share to Canada.[95]

---

[91] Department of Transportation, "Cross-Border Trucking Demonstration Project," March 11, 2008.

[92] See CRS Report RL31738, *North American Free Trade Agreement (NAFTA) Implementation: The Future of Commercial Trucking Across the Mexican Border*, by John Frittelli.

[93] Rosella Brevetti, "Key GOP House Members Urge Obama to Develop New Mexico Truck Program," *International Trade Reporter*, March 26, 2009.

[94] Amy Tsui, "Plan to Resolve Mexican Trucking Dispute 'Very Near,' DOT's LaHood Tells Lawmakers," *International Trade Reporter*, March 11, 2010.

[95] Ibid.

On August 16, 2010, the Mexican government announced a revised list of retaliatory tariffs on imports from the United States. The revised list added 26 products to and removed 16 products from the original list of 89, bringing the new total to 99 products from 43 states with a total export value of $2.6 billion. Products that were added to the list included several types of pork products, several types of cheeses, sweet corn, pistachios, oranges, grapefruits, apples, oats and grains, chewing gum, ketchup, and other products. The largest in terms of value were two categories of pork products, which had an estimated export value of $438 million in 2009. Products that were removed from the list included peanuts, dental floss, locks, and other products.[96] The revised retaliatory tariffs were lower than the original tariffs and ranged from 5% to 25%. Mexico reportedly rotated the list of products to put more pressure on the United States to seek a settlement for the trucking dispute.[97] U.S. producers of fruits, pork, cheese, and other products that were bearing the cost of the retaliatory tariffs reacted strongly at the lack of progress in resolving the trucking issue and argued, both to the Obama Administration and to numerous Members of Congress, that they were potentially losing millions of dollars in sales as a result of this dispute.

The Mexican government indicated it was willing to resolve the ongoing dispute with the Obama Administration. In March 2011, President Obama and Mexican President Calderón announced that they had agreed on a way to move forward to resolving the dispute. Mexico stated that once a final agreement was reached, it would suspend retaliatory tariffs in stages, beginning with reducing tariffs by 50% at the signing of an agreement and suspending the remaining 50% when the first Mexican carrier was granted operating authority under the program.[98] By October 2011, Mexico had suspended all retaliatory tariffs on U.S. exports to Mexico.

Obama Administration's Proposal of 2011

In January 2011, the Obama Administration presented an "initial concept document" to Congress and the Mexican government for a new long-haul trucking program with numerous safety inspection requirements for Mexican carriers. The concept document would put in place a new inspection and monitoring regime in which Mexican carriers would have to apply for long-haul operating authority. The proposed project would include several thousand trucks and eventually bring as many vehicles as are needed into the United States.[99] A DOT press release from January 6, 2011, stated that a formal proposal on which the public would have the opportunity to comment would be released in the coming months.[100] The Mexican government responded positively to the initiative, stating that it would not continue rotating the list of retaliatory tariffs, but that it would keep the current tariffs in place until a final accord was reached.[101]

---

[96] *Inside U.S. Trade's World Trade Online*, "Pork, Cheeses, Fruits to Face new Tariffs Due to Mexico Trucks Dispute," August 17, 2010.

[97] *Inside U.S. Trade's World Trade Online*, "New Mexican Retaliatory Tariffs in Trucks Dispute Designed to Spur U.S.," September 3, 2010.

[98] *Washington Trade Daily*, "A Trucking Breakthrough," Volume 20, No. 45, March 4, 2011.

[99] Rosella Brevetti and Nacha Cattan, "DOT's LaHood Presents 'Concept' Paper on Resolving NAFTA Mexico Truck Dispute," January 13, 2011.

[100] U.S. Department of Transportation, "U.S. Cross-Border Trucking Effort Emphasizes Safety and Efficiency," Press Release, January 6, 2011.

[101] Josh Mitchell, "U.S. Jump-Starts Bid to End Truck Dispute with Mexico," *Wall Street Journal*, January 7, 2011.

The U.S. concept document outlined a proposed program with three sets of elements. The first set of elements, pre-operations elements, included an application process for Mexican carriers interested in applying for long-haul operations in the United States; a vetting process by the U.S. Department of Homeland Security and the Department of Justice; a safety audit of Mexican carriers applying for the program; documentation of Mexican commercial driver's license process to demonstrate comparability to the U.S. process; and evidence of financial responsibility (insurance) of the applicant. The second set of elements, operations elements, included the following: monitoring procedures that included regular inspections and electronic monitoring of long-haul vehicles and drivers; a follow-up review (first review) to ensure continued safe operation; a compliance review (second review) upon which a participating carrier would be eligible for full operation authority; and a Federal Motor Carrier Safety Administration (FMCSA) review that included insurance monitoring and drug and alcohol collection and testing facilities. The third set of elements, transparency elements, would require Federal Register notices by the FMCSA; a publically accessible website that provides information on participating carriers; the establishment of a Federal Advisory Committee with representation from a diverse group of stakeholders; periodic reports to Congress; and requirements for DOT Office of the Inspector General reports to Congress.[102]

2011 Memorandum of Understanding to Resolve the Dispute

On July 6, 2011, the two countries signed a Memorandum of Understanding (MOU) to resolve the dispute over long-haul cross-border trucking.[103] Within 10 days after signing of the MOU, Mexico suspended 50% of the retaliatory tariffs. Mexico agreed to suspend the remainder of the tariffs within five days of the first Mexican trucking company receiving its U.S. operating authority.[104] On October 21, 2011, Mexico suspended the remaining retaliatory tariffs.

The new program, which will end in October 2014, was announced by the DOT Federal Motor Carrier Safety Administration (FMCSA). DOT Secretary LaHood stressed that roadway safety would be a priority in the program.[105] The program came as a result of numerous meetings between Secretary LaHood, other Obama Administration officials, lawmakers, safety advocates, industry representatives, and others to address concerns. According to the FMCSA, the final text of the program addresses recommendations of over 2,000 commenters to the proposal issued in April 2011.[106] Under the program, trucks will be required to comply with all Federal Motor Vehicle Safety Standards and must have electronic monitoring systems to track hours-of-service compliance. In addition, DOT is to review the complete driving record of each driver in addition to having drug testing requirements for all drivers. Other requirements include an assessment of abilities to understand the English language and U.S. traffic signs.[107] Under the new agreement,

---

[102] U.S. Department of Transportation, *Concept Document: Phased U.S.-Mexico Cross-Border Long Haul Trucking Proposal*, January 6, 2011, at http://www.fmcsa.dot.gov.

[103] Federal Motor Carrier Safety Administration (FMCSA), "United States and Mexico Announce Safe, Secure Cross-Border Trucking Program: U.S.-Mexico Agreements Will Lift Tariffs and Put Safety First," *News Release*, July 6, 2011.

[104] *NAFTA Works*, "The United States and Mexico Sign a Memorandum of Understanding on Long-Hayl Cross-Border Trucking," Volume 3, Alert 18, July 2011.

[105] FMCSA, "United States and Mexico Announce Safe, Secure Cross-Border Trucking Program: U.S.-Mexico Agreements Will Lift Tariffs and Put Safety First," July 6, 2011.

[106] Ibid.

[107] Ibid.

Mexico will provide reciprocal authority for U.S. carriers to engage in cross-border long-haul operations in Mexico.

On October 14, 2011, the FMCSA granted the first permit to provide international long-haul cargo services to Monterrey-based trucking firm Transportes Olympic. The company successfully completed a pre-authorization safety audit and had been a participant in the Bush Administration's 2007 pilot program.[108]

Policy Issues

U.S. policymakers are likely to closely follow trade issues regarding the TPP negotiations and regulatory cooperation with Mexico. They are also likely to follow ongoing economic reforms and policies implemented by the Peña Nieto government, particularly in the energy sector.

TPP Negotiations

Policy makers may consider how a TPP would affect NAFTA and U.S.-Mexico trade relations. Although nearly all U.S. trade with Mexico is now conducted duty and barrier free through NAFTA, the TPP negotiations may provide a venue for addressing issues that are not covered by NAFTA. The TPP may have implications for NAFTA in several areas, including IPR, investment, services, government procurement, as well as labor and environmental provisions. The provisions in more recent agreements that the United States has negotiated, such as the FTAs with Colombia and Peru, include commitments that go beyond NAFTA. If an agreement is reached on a TPP, Mexico may have to adhere to stronger and more enforceable labor and environmental provisions, stronger IPR provisions, as well as new rules on state-owned enterprises.[109]

Potential questions that Congress might consider include the following: If a TPP agreement is concluded, how would it affect U.S. economic relations with Mexico? How would it affect bilateral trade? Would a TPP address concerns of policymakers who believe that NAFTA's environmental and labor provisions do not go far enough to protect worker rights and the environment? Would there be an improvement in the enforcement mechanism? How would stronger IPR provisions affect U.S. industries? How would a TPP affect jobs in the United States and Mexico?

Regulatory Cooperation

Policymakers may consider issues on how the United States can improve cooperation with Mexico in the areas of trade, transportation, competitiveness, economic growth, and security enhancement. U.S.-Mexico regulatory cooperation efforts include the following: the 2010 Declaration Concerning Twenty-first Century Border Management; the 2012 High-Level Regulatory Cooperation Council (HLRCC); and the 2013 U.S.-Mexico High Level Economic Dialogue (HLED). Some policy experts emphasize the importance of U.S.-Mexico trade in

---

[108] Rosella Brevetti, "Mexico Suspends Tariffs as Trucking Program is Launched," *International Trade Reporter*, October 27, 2011.

[109] See CRS Report R42344, *Trans-Pacific Partnership (TPP) Countries: Comparative Trade and Economic Analysis*, by Brock R. Williams.

intermediate goods and supply chains and argue that the two governments can improve cooperation in cross-border trade and can invest more in improving border infrastructure. The increased security measures along the U.S.-Mexico-border, they argue, have resulted in a costly disruption in production chains due to extended and unpredictable wait times along the border.

Potential questions that Congress might consider include the following: How effectively has the United States pursued border initiatives with Mexico? What other steps can be taken by the two countries to improve competitiveness of industries located along the U.S.-Mexico border and elsewhere within the two countries? How successful have the United States and Mexico been in improving the flow of goods and services, while improving safety and security along the border? What have been the actual results of the initiatives that have been launched? To what extent has the emphasis on border security caused delays in border crossings or transportation of merchandise? How have recent efforts to facilitate trade affected the trade relationship?

Mexico's Economic Reforms

As Mexico moves forward with reform measures to modernize the energy sector and other parts of the economy, the overarching questions are how the reform agenda will be implemented; whether it will be implemented fully; and whether it will be enough to drive economic growth among all sectors of the economy, increase employment in the formal sector, and bring more people out of poverty.

Potential oversight questions that Congress might consider include the following: How effectively are the Peña Nieto government and the Mexican Congress implementing economic reforms? To what extent will the energy reforms provide opportunities for U.S. oil companies? What is the expected timeline for the energy reforms? How effective will these reforms be in bringing in more competition? Will the reforms improve Mexican economic performance? Are the secondary laws that are required to implement the constitutional reforms being carried out effectively?

Appendix. Map of Mexico

Figure A-1. Map of Mexico

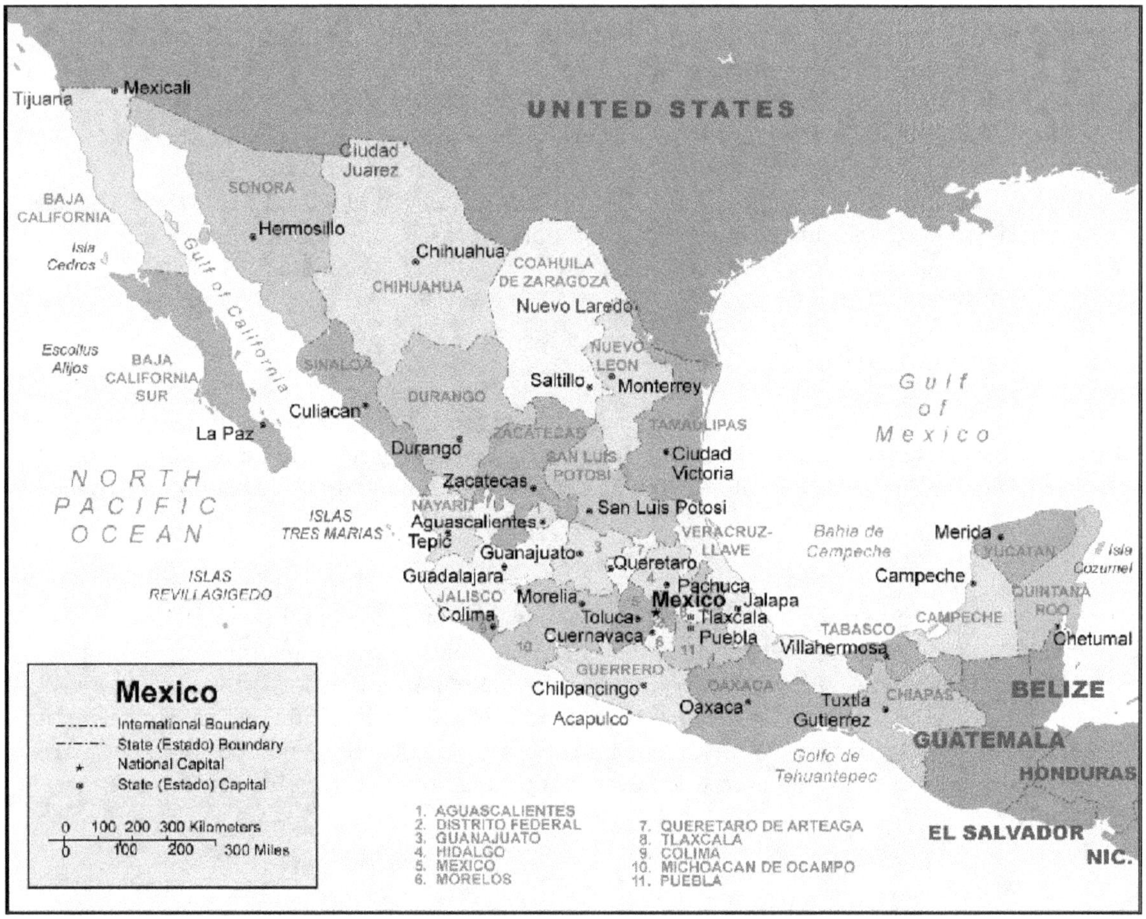

Author Contact Information

M. Angeles Villarreal
Specialist in International Trade and Finance
avillarreal@crs.loc.gov, 7-0321